A bridge ready for a white Christmas

Winter

Mary L. Meyer

SEASONS

A⁺

Smart Apple Media

B

COPYRIGHT

🖊 Published by Smart Apple Media

1980 Lookout Drive, North Mankato, MN 56003

Designed by Rita Marshall

Printed in the United States of America

🖊 Photographs by Dennis Frates, Tom Stack & Associates (Ann Duncan, Jeff Foott, John Gerlach, Thomas Kitchin, Allen B. Smith)

🖊 Library of Congress Cataloging-in-Publication Data

Meyer, Mary L. Winter / by Mary L. Meyer. p. cm. — (Seasons)

Includes bibliographical references and index.

Summary: Describes the climate and activities of winter and the ways in which some animals and plants deal with cold weather.

🖊 ISBN 1-58340-142-3

1. Winter—Juvenile literature. [1. Winter.] I. Title.

QB637.8 .M49 2002   508.2—dc21   2001049975

🖊 First Edition 9 8 7 6 5 4 3 2 1

Winter

CONTENTS

Winter Weather

Short days, long nights, chilly winds, and falling snow are signs that winter has arrived. Of all four seasons—spring, summer, fall, and winter—winter is the coldest. It lasts about three months. 🍂 The seasons change because the earth is tipped on its **axis** as it travels around the sun. In the winter, parts of the earth that are tilted away from the sun receive less sunlight. The winter sun never rises very high in the sky to warm the earth in these places. 🍂 The first day of winter in

Leaves covered with the first frost of the season

northern regions is December 21. It is also the shortest day of the year, but usually not the coldest. The coldest winter days are often in January. Most places in northern regions see snow during the winter. Snowflakes form when water in the clouds freezes into ice crystals. Snowstorms with strong winds and very cold temperatures are called blizzards. Huge drifts of snow may block roads and close schools. People use shovels, snowblowers, and plows to remove snow from sidewalks and streets. Once snow covers the ground, it may not melt until the warm winds of spring arrive.

Surviving the Cold

For many animals in northern regions, winter is a difficult time. Food and shelter are often hard to find. Some birds

Fir trees swaying in a winter wind storm

A forest coated by a heavy snowfall

migrate to escape the cold weather. In the fall, they may fly hundreds of miles to warmer places and stay there until spring.

Most animals, however, stay in one place year-round. Like a blanket, snow keeps the ground underneath it from freezing. Small, mouse-like animals, such as shrews and moles, live in underground burrows all winter. Animals such as chipmunks and groundhogs find a place to **hibernate**. They crawl into underground nests, caves, or hollow logs and sleep through the coldest months. Frogs, turtles, and

A shrew must eat its own weight in food every day to survive. Many die in winter when food is scarce.

12

salamanders hibernate in the mud at the bottom of a lake or

river. Animals that do not hibernate grow thicker coats of

fur to protect themselves from the cold. Beavers, foxes, and

A snowshoe hare dressed for winter

rabbits all grow winter coats. The winter fur of some animals is as white as snow to **camouflage** them from other animals who might harm them. While some insects, such as the monarch butterfly, migrate hundreds of miles south to warmer places for the winter, most insects simply move deeper into old logs or burrow underground.

Sleeping Plants

Plants need both sunlight and water to grow. In the winter, snow cover and fewer hours of daylight reduce the amount of sunlight that can reach plants. Cold temperatures

cause the water in the soil to freeze into ice. Plant roots cannot

absorb the frozen water. As a result, some small plants die at

the end of the growing season. Only their seeds survive the

Many birds migrate south before winter sets in

winter. 🍃 Other plants may look like they are dead, but they are actually **dormant**. Plants that live for many years store food in their roots. When winter is over, the young stems and leaves use this stored food to shoot up through the ground. Bushes and trees have thick bark that protects them from the cold and prevents them from drying out. While bushes and trees do not grow during the winter, their berries and nuts provide food for animals.

Evergreen plants have leaves in the form of waxy needles or scales so they do not dry out in the winter.

Crab apples cling to wintry branches

Winter Activities

During the winter in northern regions, many people enjoy outdoor activities such as skiing, tobogganing, ice skating, hockey, and ice fishing. Just as birds fluff their feathers to trap a warm layer of air around their bodies, people stay warm outdoors by wearing layers of clothes. 🌿 Winter holidays bring families together to celebrate their religious beliefs, exchange gifts, and eat special foods.

More than 50 percent of a person's body heat is lost through the top of the head. Wearing a hat prevents this loss.

Ice fishing is a popular winter pastime in the North

Christmas, Hanukkah, and Kwanzaa are some of the holidays celebrated during the winter months. Many cities also hold winter carnivals. An annual snow festival in Japan celebrates the beauty of snow with giant snow stat- ues and ice sculptures. While winter is a resting time for most plants and animals, it is also a wonderful time for people to bundle up and enjoy the great outdoors.

In 1959, a six-day snowstorm dumped 189 inches (480 cm) of snow on Mt. Shasta Ski Bowl in California.

Festive lights bring cheer to a cold night

Floating Snowflakes

Snowflakes fall from the sky and drift gently to the ground. This simple experiment will show you why they do not hit the earth hard like rain.

What You Need

Two pieces of notebook paper

What You Do

1. Crumple one piece of notebook paper into a small ball.
2. Place the ball of paper in one hand and the uncrumpled sheet of paper parallel to the floor in the other hand. Hold both hands at shoulder height and let the pieces of paper drop at the same time.

What You See

The ball of paper hits the floor first, and the sheet of paper floats down slowly. The ball is like a raindrop and the sheet of paper is like a snowflake—both are water, but they have different shapes. The round raindrop, like the crumpled paper, takes up a small amount of space and falls quickly. The flat paper, like a snowflake crystal, drifts to the floor because it has greater surface area.

An up-close look at a snowflake

Index

Words to Know

axis (AK-sis)—the imaginary line through the earth that connects the North and South Poles

camouflage (CAM-uh-flahj)—the use of color or shape to blend into one's surroundings

dormant (DOR-ment)—inactive or asleep

hibernate (HI-burr-nayt)—to spend the winter in a resting state

migrate (MY-grate)—to move from one area to another according to the changing seasons

Read More

Bennett, Paul. *Hibernation*. New York: Thomson Learning, 1995.

Nielsen, Nancy J. *Animal Migration*. New York: Franklin Watts, 1991.

Quiri, Patricia Ryon. *Seasons*. Minneapolis, Minn.: Compass Point Books, 2001.

Internet Sites

CNN.com In-Depth Specials: Winter Weather
http://www.cnn.com/weather/winter

The Official Groundhog Site
http://www.groundhogs.com

FEMA for Kids: Winter Storms
http://www.fema.gov/kids/wntstrm.htm